conte

For Stacy and Michele, for never letting me pay more than eight dollars for *anything*. I love you.

Special thanks to . . .
Variny Paladino for her financial expertise, enthusiasm, and dedication to empowering others with financial know-how; Mark Price and Leni Uddyback-Fortson at the U.S. Department of Labor; and Cassindy Chao, for her stock market wisdom.

nts

introduction

When it comes to money, the most powerful four-letter word you can learn isn't an obscene one. It's not one you have to mutter under your breath, or something you could never say in front of grandma.

It's *save*.

S! A! V! E! Save! Save! Save!

If you take away nothing else from this book, let it be this: Saving money may not seem fun, or especially important right now—but if you start saving money today, you could possibly become a *millionaire* over time, just by letting your savings work for you!

Curious? This book will explain how doing something as common as saving today can lead to *un*common results later. It will also suggest ways for you to *make* money, spend it wisely, use it to help others, and even deal with the sticky situations money sometimes creates.

But before we get to all of that, here are some facts:

FACT: Money can't buy happiness.

FACT: Money can't buy love.

FACT: Despite what money *can't* buy, teens in the U.S. still spend more than 100 *billion* dollars each year!

Some days, it can seem like money makes the world go 'round. You may wish you could buy the clothes your friends do, or you might feel self-conscious about what your family can't—or *can*—afford. And it's hard to go a *day* without hearing about celebrities' wild shopping sprees and big-time salaries. But whether your family spends a lot or saves a lot, is rich or poor, or somewhere in between, *you* can take control of your financial future *now* with the helpful hints in this book.

Money Matters

Sometimes, in books or movies or on TV, it can seem like the people who want a lot of money are the "bad guys." Other times, people who have money are portrayed as the luckiest, happiest people in the world. So, what's the story? Is money a bad thing, or a good thing?

The truth, as you probably guessed, is somewhere in the middle.

Money is not the answer to all of life's problems. Greed can cloud people's judgment and make them do irresponsible things. But money also isn't something to feel bad about wanting or having. Money *does* matter. Because with money come opportunities, freedom, and choice. For example:

- **Making and saving your own money can build your confidence and earn you respect from your parents, friends, and guys, as well as more independence for yourself.**

- **Money can open the door to opportunities, like a college education, travel, and—yes—the thrill of treating yourself to cool stuff!**

- **Money can give you the power to change and improve your life, and the lives of others.**

Of course, as your money grows, it's important to make sure that it, and the power that comes with it, doesn't change who you are and the values you hold important. Luckily, *The Teen Girl's Gotta-Have-It Guide to Money* is here to help you stay grounded. So read on, pay attention, and let the lessons here guide you wherever your bank account takes you!

The Teen Girl's Gotta-Have-It RULES for Minding Your Money, AKA: W.A.L.L.E.T.

Here are six golden rules to keep in mind as you make your money wishes come true.

WORK Working will not only give you spending and saving money, but it will make you a more impressive candidate when you apply to college. Also, it will teach you skills beyond what you could ever learn at school. Just be sure to talk to your parents before getting any kind of job.

plan AHEAD Think beyond the moment to your goals for next month, next year, and four years from now. Then use the tips in this book to create a money plan and stick to it. Planning ahead means you'll be less likely to *waste* your money.

LOVE something When you're passionate about something—school, art, music, fashion, *anything*—you can make it a priority and spend money on the things that matter most to you.

LET your money work for you Don't just leave your savings in a piggy bank or shoebox at home. When you put your money in a savings account or make another type of investment, it will start earning money *for* you!

EXPLORE your spending options What's the secret to making smart shopping decisions? Checking out all of your options by doing research and asking around. Especially with bigger purchases, it pays to take your time.

TOUCH lives When you make your budget, consider setting aside some money to give to charity. You don't have to give a *lot* of money to make a difference.

show me

the money!

The first step in your money plan is to *make* some in the first place!

But where to begin? Well, with this chapter of course. It'll give you ideas about what kind of jobs are out there, prep you for writing your first résumé, and provide you with tips on how to ace your first job interview.

Working isn't *just* about making money. It's also about learning new things, meeting people, developing skills, and gaining confidence and independence. When you work, you gain access to a whole new world.

There's a job out there for *everyone,* and the best job for you is one doing something that really interests you. So don't just stick to the ideas in this chapter. Think of what *you* want to do. If you have an idea, share it with an adult you trust (like a parent or guidance counselor) and discuss ways to make it happen. When you pursue work you feel passionate about, you'll get *way* more out of your job than just a paycheck. And remember: Any job you get will look great on your college application. It will show that you're responsible, self-reliant, and thinking about your future.

Wanted:
Reliable
Babysitter
Call Mrs. Brown
ww-ww

Cat Sitter
Needed
Immediately!

Call Julie
ww-ww

PART-TIME
STUDENT HELP
NEEDED!

APPLY WITHIN
with Resume

What Kind of Job Should You Get?

START HERE

Risks:

THRILL ME → **I am good at making decisions.**

SCARE ME → **I like sports that require:**

FALSE → **At school clubs, I like to:**

INDIVIDUAL SUCCESS

TEAMWORK

TRUE → **Around parents and adults I'm:**

RUN THE SHOW

SHOW UP AND PITCH IN → **I'm always dreaming about:**

TALKATIVE AND COMFORTABLE

SHY AND QUIET

LIFE AFTER COLLEGE

COLLEGE

START YOUR OWN BUSINESS You're confident when it comes to taking charge, and you're comfortable talking to adults and people in authority. You also welcome the challenges that come with taking risks. So consider starting your own business and being your own boss using the tips on the next few pages. Or if you decide to work for someone *else*, soak up all the knowledge and experience you can so that someday you can take on a leadership position within an existing company or at a company you start.

APPLY FOR AN EXISTING JOB You enjoy being a part of a group and welcome the structure that teams and school offer, which means you'll be a valuable member of any staff, and a boss would be lucky to have you as an employee! Seek out jobs that exist around town, like the jobs starting on page 20. And remember that, sometimes, taking a small risk or pushing yourself out of your comfort zone just a *little* bit can yield *big* rewards. Use the routine and familiarity of a formal job setting to try new things, develop new skills, and build your confidence when it comes to talking with adults and speaking up for yourself.

The Rules

Before you can get on the road to working, you have to know the rules.

There's a government organization called the Department of Labor (www.dol.gov) that oversees a law called The Fair Labor Standards Act (FLSA). This law states what kinds of jobs you can do if you're under 18, how many hours you can work, and the minimum wage that you can be paid. According to the FLSA, here's the scoop:

IF YOU'RE 13 OR YOUNGER, you can do these jobs:

- Deliver newspapers

- Act for a modeling or acting agency

- Work for yourself doing things like babysitting, pet-walking, shoveling snow, and so on

- Work for your parents' business or farm (unless they own a business that deals with manufacturing, mining, or any other work the government considers "hazardous").

IF YOU'RE 14, you can do the jobs listed above, as well as work at retail stores, gas stations, and food establishments. The number of hours you can work depends on the time of year:

During the school year, you can work after school for three hours per day, or on weekends for eight hours per day. You *cannot* work more than 18 hours per week, or before 7AM or after 7PM.

During summer vacation (from June 1 through Labor Day), you can work between 7AM and 9PM, but you cannot work more than 40 hours per week.

IF YOU'RE 16 OR 17, you can do pretty much any job except what the government considers "hazardous." This is not as obvious as you'd think. To get a complete list, check out YouthRules! at www.youthrules.dol.gov. There are no limits as to when or for how long you can work.

In addition to these national laws, each *state* has its own rules about the kinds of jobs you can get. To find out your state's rules, visit www.youthrules.dol.gov or call 866-4US-WAGE. Some states also might require a work permit or age certificate before you can apply for a job. Ask your school's guidance counselor if this applies to your state, and if so, how to apply for one.

secrets of success

Save yourself time! Before you fill out *any* job application, find out (from your school or employer) the minimum age requirement for the job.

What are taxes, and do I have to pay them?

Everyone in the United States who makes more than a certain amount of money (about $5,150, though this number can change from year to year) is required by law to pay money to the U.S. government.

This is a tax on your *income,* or the money you earn, and is called *income* tax. This money helps pay for things like roads, schools, and the police force.

If you're working for a company, business, or store, you will be asked to fill out a form called a W-4, and taxes will automatically be taken from your paycheck. Depending on how much money you make, you might still have to pay more taxes on top of the money that's taken from your check.

If you're working as your own boss, you will have to pay the taxes yourself. The amount you have to earn in order to owe taxes changes every year. If you've made even *close* to $5,000 in one calendar year, ask a parent. To find out if you have to pay income tax and how much you have to pay, go to www.irs.gov/app/understandingTaxes.

Work for Yourself

Now that you know the rules, it's time to start making some dough! The first step is to figure out if you want to work for yourself or someone else.

Working for yourself means that you get to be your own boss, and that you get the freedom to make all your own choices. But it also means loads of responsibility, as everything depends on *you*. If you're ready to strike out on your own here are some ideas. But if you think you'd prefer to work for someone else, check pages 20–21.

JOB	WHAT IT INVOLVES	HOW TO CHARGE	HELPFUL HINTS
Acting or performing for fun	Putting on your own plays or concerts	Per ticket	Ask your parents for permission before you invite people to your house to see your show.
Babysitting	Taking care of children	By the hour	If possible, enroll in a babysitting class at your local hospital before you start working.
Cleaning houses	Dusting, mopping, vacuuming, and doing other chores to clean a person's home	By the hour	Wear protective gloves and inexpensive sneakers so you don't ruin a nice pair.
Dog walking	Taking a dog (or dogs) out for walks in your neighborhood	By the day or week	Before you take the job, find out if the dog is kid-friendly and if it has any allergies or quirks.
Gardening	Taking care of the lawns and/or gardens of your neighbors	By the week or day	Don't forget to wear sunscreen (and it wouldn't hurt to learn something about gardening!)

JOB	WHAT IT INVOLVES	HOW TO CHARGE	HELPFUL HINTS
Giving makeovers	Doing makeup and/or hair for clients	By the session	Use disposable applicators, like cotton swabs and cotton balls.
Party helping	Helping out at children's birthday parties	A fee per party, based on what you're expected to do	Offer to take pictures at the party, and charge for that service, too!
Pet sitting	Caring for a pet while its owner is away	By the day or week	Be clear that you'll need to charge more if you have to pay for things like food or supplies.
Shoveling snow or raking leaves	Clearing snow or leaves off walkways and driveways of homes in your neighborhood	One fee for walkways, one for driveways, and one for extra-long driveways	Only leave fliers within walking distance. After a big snowstorm, your parents may not be able to drop you off!
Starting a fashion business	Making clothes and accessories and selling them to others, In person or online	A set price for each item	Host a fashion show at your home, with your friends as models. (But make sure to get your parents' permission first!)
Tutoring	Helping students with subjects they would like to do better in— and that you know very well	By the hour	Always take time to prepare before each tutoring session.
Writing	Writing poetry, fiction, or nonfiction and submitting it for publication	Different publications pay by the word, by the story, or article . . . or not at all	Ask your English teacher to help you find publications and contests open to student writers.

Taking Care of Business

Okay, you have an idea for your business . . . now what? Here are some tips for starting your business and keeping it going.

SPREAD THE WORD. Tell your family and friends about your business, and ask them to spread the word. You can also put flyers in your neighbors' mailboxes and around your neighborhood, saying exactly what you do and how to contact you. Check with your parents first, to make sure you can give out your contact information. You may want to create a new e-mail address for your business, with a name like "MathWhiz" or "#1Babysitter."

BE CLEAR WITH CLIENTS. Whenever you get a new client, agree on a clear list of your tasks and responsibilities before you start the job. If you're babysitting, are you expected to cook dinner? If you're giving a makeover, does your client get to keep the makeup?

TALK MONEY—BEFORE YOU START WORKING. Discussing money can be awkward, but it's important to agree on a fair fee *before* you start working for a new client. You can use the "going rate" (what your friends earn) in your town as a starting point, or you may want to use the minimum wage (or a few dollars more than it) as a suggested starting point for an hourly wage. To find out your state's minimum wage, go to www.dol.gov/esa/minwage/america.htm.

GIVE RECEIPTS. If you're selling something, decide in advance what your policy will be on returns. Give each customer some kind of receipt with the following information: what they bought, how much they paid, the date, and your return policy.

BE PREPARED FOR AN EMERGENCY.

Any time you're caring for others, as with babysitting or dog walking, ask your client for a list of emergency phone numbers so you can contact them quickly if anything should happen.

THINK AHEAD IF YOU'LL BE GOING AWAY.

If you know you'll be going out of town, let your clients know as soon as possible so they can make other plans for the time you'll be away.

BUILD UP A LIST OF REFERENCES.

Ask clients whether they'd be willing to give a reference for you to future employers and/or future clients.

Emergency List

Work: ⁓⁓⁓⁓

Neighbor: ⁓⁓ ⁓⁓

Friend: ⁓⁓⁓⁓

Police: ⁓⁓⁓⁓

911

secrets of success

Make your own business cards! Pick up a template and a set of blank cards at an office supply store. Then follow the directions to set them up on your computer. Ask a parent what to put on your cards—they may want you to list only an e-mail address and not a phone number, or vice versa.

My Business Card
email: me@my email.com
dogwalking & pet-sitting

Work for Someone Else

The beauty of working for someone else is that you don't bear the burden of finding customers or minding the costs.

Plus, you get to meet people and learn from those with more experience. Sometimes these jobs even offer perks, like company discounts. The downside, for some people, is that you have to play by your boss's rules and stick to someone else's schedule.

TYPE OF BUSINESS	JOBS AVAILABLE	MINIMUM AGE	HOW IT PAYS	HELPFUL HINTS
Acting or modeling agency	Professional modeling and acting jobs	None	Depends on the job	Beware of agencies that charge a fee up-front. Most legitimate agencies won't charge you until they find you a job.
Grocery store	Cashier, bagger, and shelf stocker	14	By the hour	Wear comfortable shoes. You'll probably be on your feet all day!
Local newspaper	Delivering the paper to subscribers in a specific neighborhood	None	A daily rate	Check the weather report each night so you can plan what to wear.
Movie theater	Ticket seller, usher, or concession stand worker	14	By the hour	Don't assume you can watch movies for free—ask your supervisor first!
Office or business	Office assistant	14–16*	By the hour	Prepare a résumé before applying (see page 26).

*14 in retail, food service, gasoline service establishments, and government offices; otherwise 16

TYPE OF BUSINESS	JOBS AVAILABLE	MINIMUM AGE	HOW IT PAYS	HELPFUL HINTS
Private and public pools and beaches	Lifeguard *15 with Red Cross or equivalent certification at a pool; 16 at a beach	15-16*	By the hour	All lifeguards must take a class and be certified by the American Red Cross (www.redcross.org).
Restaurant	Busperson, cashier, prep cook, and many other jobs *14 to work as a busperson, cashier, or host; 16 to be a prep cook	14-16*	By the hour, possibly, plus a share of the tips	If you have to wear a uniform, ask in advance whether you'll have to pay for it.
Retail store	Cashier or salesperson	14	By the hour	Apply at stores that you love. You'll enjoy the job more!
Summer camp	Counselor, counselor-in-training, or lifeguard* *see Lifeguard entry above	14-16	A flat fee for the summer season	For more information, see the American Camp Association's website at www.aca-camps.org.
Theater company	Prop or set builder *18 to use certain power tools	16-18*	A flat fee for the play	Read the script of the play so you understand what's going on around you.

secrets of success

Don't see anything you like? How about working at the zoo, assisting at a nursery school, or scooping ice cream? There are *tons* of jobs out there. The first step in trying to get one is figuring out where you would like to work. Then you should check out the business's website, call them, or just stop in to find out if they're hiring.

Happy Hunting

Here are some ways to start looking for a job in your area.

NETWORK. Your family and friends are great sources of information. Tell them you're looking for a new job—they may know people who are looking for help!

FILL OUT AN APPLICATION. If you want to work at a restaurant or store, stop by during quiet times. Restaurants are slow on weekdays in the late afternoons, before the dinner rush. For stores, slow times include early weekend mornings and late weekday evenings. Ask to speak with the manager or owner. Introduce yourself, and ask if they are hiring and if you can fill out an application. You can also leave a copy of your résumé. (See sample résumé on page 26.)

CHECK COMPANY WEBSITES. Search the Internet for the company you're interested in working for, and surf their website to find employment opportunities. Usually the department that handles hiring is called "Human Resources" or "Personnel." Although they may not list jobs for teens on their site, you can e-mail the Human Resources department to find out what opportunities may exist for you.

VISIT STUDENT JOB SITES. You can also check out student job sites like www.studentjobs.gov or other job databases—just make sure your parents approve of the sites.

KEEP YOUR EYES OPEN. Be on the lookout for postings in cafés, community centers, and your school's guidance office.

Wanted!
Reliable
Babysitter
Call Mrs. Brown
\\\\-\\\\

Cat Sitter
Needed
Immediately!

Call Julie
\\\\-\\\\

PART-TIME
STUDENT HELP
NEEDED!

APPLY WITHIN
with Resume

Interviewing 101

Once you find a job to go after, you'll want to make a positive first impression. Here are some tips to help you ace job interviews.

GETTING READY

Do your homework. If the business has a website, check it out. Small, local businesses might not always have websites—but you can still do an online search to try to find out more about the company, the kind of business it does, and the people who work for it. Doing research will help you ask smart, informed questions—and will also help you figure out if the company's a good match for you.

Do a trial run. Ask a parent or friend if you can practice doing an interview, even if it might feel corny. Sit face-to-face and explain why you think you're the perfect fit for the job that you're applying for—tell them about your strengths, interests, and passion for that particular job. Ask your partner to tell you if you were fidgeting or saying things such as "like" or "um." Keep practicing until you work out any kinks.

Prepare a résumé. As a teenager, you probably won't be *expected* to have a résumé —but that's all the more reason why having one will make you stand out as a great candidate for a job! And even if you don't have much—or any—job experience, you can still put together a résumé. A résumé is really just a summary of your contact information, goals, skills, and references. Check out the sample on page 26, and adapt it for you.

INTERVIEW DAY!

Dress appropriately. Dress as neatly as possible. Wear pants or a knee-length skirt, and be sure you're not showing any belly, a thong, or too much skin! Keep your hair off your face. If you wear makeup, keep it to a minimum.

Bring a pen and paper. Show up with a notebook and pen so you can write down information and questions that come to mind before the interview, while you're in it, or afterward.

Don't chew gum. 'Nuff said! If you're worried about having bad breath, pop a mint into your mouth on your way to the interview.

Turn off your cell phone. Be sure to turn it off *before* you head into your interview.

Make eye contact. Try not to look down or around the room. Look the interviewer in the eye. If you start to feel awkward, jot some notes down in your notebook.

Listen up. Asking questions is important, but never interrupt the person interviewing you. Let him or her finish talking, no matter how excited you get about what is being said.

Ask questions. When the interviewer is done, he or she will most likely ask whether *you* have any questions. Use that time to ask a question about the type of work you'd be doing, the boss's expectations, and anything else that came to mind while the interviewer was speaking.

Have a firm handshake. Using your right hand, firmly grip the other person's hand and shake briefly. A firm handshake shows that you're confident and outgoing. Don't have a limp grasp or hold onto the other person's hand for too long.

AFTER THE INTERVIEW

Send a thank-you note. Immediately following your interview, send a thank-you note to the interviewer. If you've already had e-mail contact with him or her, send a brief message like the one below. Then, send along a handwritten note. It may seem repetitive, but taking the time to handwrite *and* e-mail a note is always impressive—and worth the extra effort.

> Dear [the interviewer's name],
>
> Thank you for taking the time to meet with me about the [insert job title] job. Learning about the position made me even more interested, and I hope you'll strongly consider me for it.
>
> Please feel free to call me with any questions. I look forward to hearing from you, and I hope you have a nice day.
>
> Thank you,
> [your name]

family affair

If you want a job that's too far away to walk to, check with your parents before applying for it to make sure that someone will be able to drive you to work and back. You can also ask your employer if there are any staff carpools, but always check with a parent before accepting a ride from anyone.

SAMPLE RÉSUMÉ:

Jane Doe
12345 Job-Hunter Street
Working, NY 12345
Phone: 555-555-5555   E-mail: janedoe@email.com

OBJECTIVE:

Insert one sentence describing the type of job you're looking for. Here are some examples:
To find a part-time job working with animals.
To apply my love of fashion to a position at *Fashion Girl*.
To learn more about cycling by getting a job at The Bike Shop.
To work as an usher at The Big Apple Movie Theater.

EXPERIENCE & ACTIVITIES:

List the job title or type of job you held, and explain in a sentence what the nature of your job was and what kinds of skills it helped you develop.

Babysitter For the past three months, I have been responsible for the safety and well-being of my siblings after school. This has taught me to be dependable, punctual, responsible, patient, and fair.

School Newspaper Reporter For three semesters, I reported on events for the sports section of my school newspaper. This taught me to work under tight deadlines and work well in groups.

Student Dancer For six years, I have been involved with local dance groups. As a serious hobby, dancing has shown me how to balance outside interests with my schoolwork and family obligations.

SKILLS:

In one sentence, list the personality traits that relate to the job you're applying for. In another sentence, list any technical skills you may have— like languages you speak or computer programs you know.

I am responsible, hardworking, punctual, and eager to learn new skills.
I am passionate about animals and hope to someday have a career working with them.
I know how to work in computer programs like Microsoft Word and am comfortable using the Internet. I also understand and speak a basic level of French.

REFERENCES:

List two adults you are not related to but who will speak highly of you. Make sure you tell the people you list that they might be receiving a call about your credentials; that way, they can prepare what they'll say in advance, and they won't be caught off-guard at the last minute.

Mrs. Smith, 8th Grade Teacher, America Junior High School, 555-555-5555

Mr. Apple, 7th Grade Basketball Coach, Town Basketball League, 555-555-5555

On-the-Job Excellence

Congratulations—you got the job! Here are some tips to keep you in the Employee Hall of Fame.

BE ON TIME. Always arrive at least five minutes early, and call your supervisor if you're ever running late.

DRESS THE PART. Wear clean clothes and keep your hair and nails looking neat.

RESPECT YOUR SCHEDULE. It's important not to let a job get in the way of your schoolwork or family life, but you also need to respect your job responsibilities. If you find out you'll have to miss work for school or family-related reasons, let your supervisor know *right away* so he or she can find someone to cover for you.

SPEAK UP. If you're ever put in an awkward position, or if you experience something that seems shady or illegal, *don't keep it to yourself*. Tell a supervisor or someone in the Human Resources department, and share your thoughts with a parent *immediately*.

TURN OFF YOUR CELL. Unless the company you're working for specifically says it's OK, don't use your phone (or e-mail or text-messaging) during work time.

GET THE FULL STORY. Most employers have an employee manual that outlines rules for the job. Ask your supervisor to see it.

One-Day Events

Another way to make money is by organizing a one-time-only event. If that's more your style, here are some ideas!

TYPE OF EVENT	WHAT IT INVOLVES	HOW TO CHARGE	HELPFUL HINTS
Bake sale	Baking sweets and then selling them	A set price for each treat	If sales start slowly, offer a "Buy 2, get 1 free!" deal.* *see "Know the rules" on page 30*
Car wash	Working with others to clean people's cars	A set fee per car	Use a gentle liquid soap and the softest sponges possible to avoid unintentional scratches.
Craft sale	Making crafts and offering them for sale	A set price for each item, or each category (such as, "All necklaces are $10!")	Take photos of everything before customers arrive. They may someday come in handy for an art portfolio.
Family garage sale	Working with your family to sort through stuff you don't need anymore, and then selling it	A set price for each item, or have a $5 table, a $10 table, and so on	If you're unsure about selling something, *don't do it*. Better to wait than to sell it and regret it later.

Running the Show

Here are some tips to make sure your event goes smoothly.

FIND A LOCATION. Decide whether to hold the sale at someone's house or in a public place. If you do it at someone's house, make sure a parent gives permission and will be around that day. *Never host an event without adult supervision.*

To hold the sale in a public space, such as a school or church, call around to see if there is a local event coming up where you could hold it, like a neighborhood block party or a school swim meet. When calling a new place, ask for the manager or building supervisor. Explain that you're a local student looking to hold a sale with your friends and want to find out whether you can have it in their facility. Make sure you find out what their cleanup policy is and whether you'll need to bring your own table and chairs. Some places might be more willing to let you sell things if some of the money you raise will go to charity.

CHOOSE YOUR TEAM. A big event can be stressful, so make sure the people you work with are trustworthy, dependable, punctual, and hardworking. You don't all need to have the same skills—but you should have the same work ethic.

SET THE PRICES. To set your prices, consider your costs and how much you need to charge to make a profit. But don't aim *too* high—if your goods are too expensive, it may turn customers away.

$25

AGREE ON A MONEY PLAN. Decide *in advance* whether you and your friends will divide the money evenly, or get paid only for the items you made that sell.

HAVE CHANGE. Before your event, stop by the bank to get change. You'll need plenty of single dollar bills and a roll each of quarters, nickels, and dimes. (You may need to borrow money from a parent before your event, but promise to pay it back immediately after— and throw in a free treat, too!)

CHECK THE WEATHER. If your event will be outdoors, set a rain date—or have an alternate, indoor location.

KNOW THE RULES. Your town may have restrictions on food sales or other events; call your Town Hall to find out.

BAKE SALE TODAY!

Cha-ching!

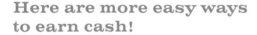

Here are more easy ways to earn cash!

ENTER CONTESTS. Talk to your teachers about essay contests, science fairs, art shows, and more.

DO YOUR CHORES. Your parents may already give you an allowance. If not, or if you want to negotiate for more, offer to take on more chores.

RECYCLE. Recycling is not only good for the environment—it can also be lucrative! Ask your parents if you can round up your family's cans, glass, plastic, and newspapers to redeem at your local supermarket or town's recycling center.

CLIP COUPONS. Coupons aren't just for grannies. Each week, when coupons come in the mail or with the newspaper, clip the ones for products your family uses. Then, ask your parents if for each dollar you save your family, you can have 50 cents. It may not seem like a lot, but if you save your family $40, you'll get $20—for not a lot of work.

A FINAL NOTE

Working won't feel like a chore if you figure out what kind of job is best for *you*. Think outside the box to find a job you'll enjoy.

Doing something you like, meeting new people, learning skills for the future, and earning your own money—it's all waiting for you!

a square

deal

Once you start making your own money, what are you going to *do* with it?

Your first instinct might be to run out and *spend* it, but it pays (*literally*) to come up with a plan that goes beyond "make money, then . . . buy stuff!"

You already know that you can use money to buy things. So obviously "spending" will be part of your plan. But what about putting some money aside for big ticket items like that pair of boots you've been eyeing? And what about longer-term goals, like buying a car, or paying for college? You might also want to help others by giving a portion to charity.

What you do with your money is a personal decision. It should be guided by *your* values, goals, family, and future plans. But whoever you are and however much money you make, there's no denying that having a plan—instead of just winging it— will help you now and in the future. This chapter will help you come up with a plan.

The Rule of Four

You know that expression, "It's hip to be square"? Well, it's also hip to *think* square— that is, to think of the money you have as a grid divided into four squares:

1. **Spending money** (as in lunch, lip gloss, or a movie).
2. **Money you're saving for short-term goals** (like that pair of boots).
3. **Money you're saving for long-term goals** (like a car or college).
4. **Money you're putting aside for charity.**

Spending
This is the money you "give" yourself to spend freely right now.

Saving
(Short-term)
This is money you're saving for something specific in the short term, meaning in the next few months. You could put this money in a savings account and withdraw it when you reach a certain goal.

Saving
(Long-term)
This is money you'll put aside for your future, possibly in one of the investments you'll learn about later. You won't use it for anything other than big things like college (or other major purchases you plan with your parents).

Charity
This is money to give to an organization of your choosing— like a dog shelter, children's hospital, environmental group, local church, synagogue, or youth recreation center. *Whatever* your passion or values, there's an organization that can use your financial help!

How *much* should you put in each square? That part of the plan is up to you. One suggestion is to put 30% of your money into spending, 30% into short-term savings, 30% into long-term savings, and 10% to go to charity.

Imagine you got $100 from your grandma for your birthday. Using a plan like this, you would divide it as follows:

Spending
30%

Take $30 and spend it on a movie with your friends and a cute new T-shirt!

Saving
(Short-term)
30%

Put $30 in your savings account until you've saved enough for those new boots. Then take the money out and go buy them!

Saving
(Long-term)
30%

With the help of your parents, put $30 aside for investing in stocks or bonds, and agree to leave it there until it's time to go to college.

Charity
10%

Donate $10 to the animal shelter where you fell in love with that adorable puppy.

See how much more you were able to do with $100 than buy only *one* thing? With just $100, you were able to treat yourself, plan for your future, and help others.

You can come up with your own version of this plan, or adapt it as your goals and needs change. For example, if you're eager to save for something you really want, maybe you'll put more in your short-term-savings square and less in the spending square for a few months. What matters isn't how *much* you put into each square, but that you keep all four squares in mind each time you earn or are given money.

Giving Back

Want to support a charity but not sure how to do so?

Start by making a list of things that are important to you—your list can be general and say things like "animals" or "reading," or it can be specific and include things like, "help protect endangered animals" or "help teach children to read."

Once you have your list, sit down with a parent to talk about finding local, national, or international organizations that support related causes. A good place to start is your public library, which has online databases and books about different charities.

When you pick a charity, make sure to find out how the organization will use your money. What portion goes to the cause itself? And what portion goes to running the charity? Ideally, you want as much of your donation as possible to go directly to the cause.

secrets of success

Giving to charity is a personal decision. Some people prefer to give *time* rather than money. Only you can decide whether and how you'd like to give. If you do decide to donate money, make sure to get a receipt. Your parents may be able to use it to pay a little less on their taxes.

A FINAL NOTE

Having a plan will help make your money go farther—also, it will help ensure that you think about what you really want, and have a strategy for how to get the money to achieve it.

Talk to your parents about the best strategy for getting the most out of *your* money—then try as hard as you can to stick to your plan.

being a

savvy saver

When it comes to dealing with money, spending is the easy part—it's *saving* that can be tricky! It can be hard to stick to your plan or stay disciplined, especially since your earnings and goals are likely to change.

The good news is that becoming a savvy saver doesn't have to stress you out or drive you bonkers. It can actually be *fun*—and make you feel empowered and in control—to plan ahead. See, becoming a smart saver doesn't mean having to *deprive* yourself— it means thinking about all the things you *want,* and then ranking them in the order they matter to you.

Ready to learn more? Then turn the page!

The Long and the Short of It

The best way to manage your savings is to think about your savings *goals*. In other words, what do you want to be able to buy?

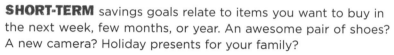

It's best to divide your savings goals into two kinds: *short-term* and *long-term*.

SHORT-TERM savings goals relate to items you want to buy in the next week, few months, or year. An awesome pair of shoes? A new camera? Holiday presents for your family?

LONG-TERM savings goals build toward bigger things for your future, and may be several years or more away, like a car, a spring break trip, or college tuition.

Your Short-Term Savings

Let's start with your short-term goals. This is the fun part!

Think about all the things you want to buy in the next week, month, or year. Then write them in the "Wish List" below. Make your best guess as to how much each item will cost.

My Wish List

ITEM	COST	RANK

When you're done, go back and look at your list again. Which item is the *most* important to you? Put a "1" next to it in the "Rank" column. Which is the *next* most important? Give it a "2." Keep going until you have ranked all the items in order of importance. Congratulations, you now have your new savings goals!

Reaching the Goal

Now that you have your #1 short-term savings goal, you're probably wondering *how long* it will take you to reach it. Here is an easy way to find out.

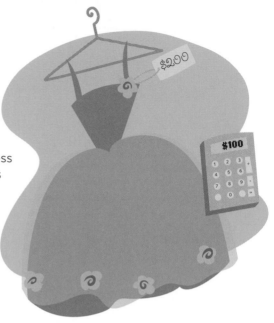

Imagine you want a prom dress that costs $200. Your parents agree to pay for half of it. That means you need to save up $100. Ask yourself these two questions to figure out how long it will take to reach this goal:

1. **How much do you need to save?** You need $100 to buy the dress.

2. **How much will you put in your short-term savings square each month?** Let's say you make $100 each month, and put aside 25% of that for short-term savings. You're saving $25 a month.

Now divide your goal (the answer to #1) by the amount you save each month (the answer to #2). **$100 \div 25 = 4$.** It will take you four months to save $100 and buy the dress.

But what if four months is too long? There are two ways to speed the process. You can *earn more,* perhaps by babysitting more often, and put the extra earnings in your savings square. Or you can *save more* by dipping into

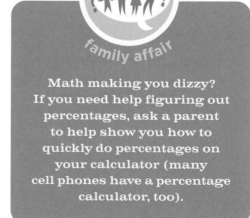

family affair

Math making you dizzy? If you need help figuring out percentages, ask a parent to help show you how to quickly do percentages on your calculator (many cell phones have a percentage calculator, too).

GO GENERIC. You don't have to buy brand-name items—especially when it comes to cosmetics and toiletries. Sometimes, the ingredients in the generic versions of things like zit creams, shampoo, and moisturizer are exactly the same as the brand-name versions. You're just paying more for the fancy packaging and expensive advertising!

TAKE CARE OF YOUR CLOTHES. If you hang up or fold your clothes at the end of the day instead of letting them pile up in the corner, they'll last longer and look better.

DO YOUR OWN NAILS. Instead of having professional manicures or pedicures, polish your own nails, or have a friend do it for you.

WATCH YOUR CELL PLAN. If you have a cell phone, find out all of your plan's details. Sometimes, if you talk at certain times of day or send more text messages than your plan covers, you can rack up lots of extra fees. Also, avoid calling the operator for information unless that service is included in your cell phone plan. Instead, look the number up online, or use the phone book. If you're responsible for paying the bill, these simple changes can really help save you money; and if your parents cover the bill, they'll appreciate your efforts (and you'll be learning what to do for the future, when you'll be in charge!).

BOTTLE YOUR OWN WATER. Instead of buying bottled water all the time, get a cute reusable water bottle and fill it up at the sink or water fountain when you're thirsty. (Make sure your bottle is dishwasher-safe so you can keep it clean and free of germs.)

HAVE A SNACK STASH. Keep snacks from home in your backpack—it's often a lot cheaper than buying them from vending machines or convenience stores.

your spending money and saving it instead (use the tips on pages 45–47 to lower your spending). Or you can do both!

Let's say you decide to cut back on your spending and put $25 of your spending money into saving for your dress instead. Now try the calculation again:

1. **How much do you need to save?** $100.

2. **How much will you put into your savings square each month?** You normally put in $25 each month. Now you're going to add $25 of your spending money, too. So the total is $50.

Divide #1 by #2. **100 ÷ 50 = 2.**

Now it will take only *two* months to save for your dress—but that's only if you don't spend that money on *anything else*. If you spend your short-term savings on other things on your Wish List, or on things you didn't plan for but that just come up, it will take longer to reach your goal.

secrets of success

It can be hard to stay focused on your savings plan. But a good way to stay on track with your goals is to remind yourself why you're saving in the first place. A few tricks are to make lists of the things you're saving for, or cut out pictures of your dream college or car and tape them into your journal or above your desk. You can also make planning for the future more fun by checking out the savings calculator at **www.jumpstartcoalition.org/realitycheck.**

Your Long-Term Savings

What about your long-term savings goals? These are the big expenses for your future, like in the next 5-10 years. They may seem far off, but they really aren't!

For example, what kind of college, school, or university do you hope to go to after high school? Will you have to pay for all or part of it? And what about transportation? Do you want to get your driver's license? And if you get one, will you want to buy a car? Will you be given a car but have to pay for gas and insurance?

Think about all the big things you dream of having for your future and write them below. If you know how much you'll be expected to contribute for each, write that down too.

My Future Wish List

ITEM	HOW MUCH YOU WILL CONTRIBUTE

These kinds of expenses are too big to save for in a few weeks or months—they are things you'll want to save for in the long term. The best way to do that is to work with a parent to put the money you set aside in a savings account or investment (more on that later) and *leave it there.* Don't touch it or use it—just keep adding to it. Whenever your motivation even starts to feel unsteady, look back at this list and remember how important these things are to your future!

Everyday Savings Tips

In addition to saving the money you earn and get as allowance and gifts, you can start to form smart habits to spend less and make your money go farther. Whether you do these all the time, or just when your savings needs an extra boost, here's how:

RESIST IMPULSE BUYS. When you go shopping and see something you like, don't buy it on the spot. Wait a couple of days, then see if you still want it.

GET THE SCOOP ON SALES. Before you buy something expensive, like a dress or shoes, ask the salesperson if it will be going on sale soon or if there are any coupons or special discounts coming out. Don't be shy—lots of people ask about sales.

SHOP AT THRIFT AND SECONDHAND STORES. You'll be surprised by the variety and quality of their goods, and you'll love the price tags!

CUT OUT THE GIANT POPCORN. Eating at the movies adds up. Candy and soda can cost up to *five* times more than at the supermarket! Eat or drink before the movie starts—or, if your theater allows it, bring snacks from home. Try hosting movie nights with your friends—it will be a lot cheaper to rent a DVD and make your own food than to each pay for a ticket. (Plus, you can sit around watching in your jammies!)

KEEP YOUR WALLET ORGANIZED. When you take care of your money, you'll be more likely to spend it wisely. If you don't have a wallet, get one. Keep your wallet organized by putting together all your dollar bills, fives, tens, twenties, and so on.

COLLECT YOUR CHANGE. Any time you have loose change, put it in one place (for example in a jar, can, or piggy bank) instead of leaving it all over your room. At the end of every month, put that money toward short- or long-term savings. Many banks have machines that will sort change for you.

A FINAL NOTE

Saving your money can be challenging—but is very rewarding. You can make simple changes in your everyday habits to save more money. However, the most important step you can take is to think today about your savings goals for the future.

Write your savings goals down in a journal or on a separate piece of paper—when you write down and keep track of your savings goals, you'll be more likely to achieve them than if you just keep them in the back of your mind.

making money

your
grow

You know how you can plant a seed, and with just a bit of care it will start to grow? Well, you can do the same thing with your money.

You can make it grow simply by putting it in the right place. Welcome to the power of investing!

Investing means taking your money and entrusting it to a bank (or a business or the government). You hope that it will *appreciate,* or make more money for you. There are lots of ways to invest your money—some are super-safe and some are risky. This chapter will explain three main ways to invest, tell you how risky each one is, and help you choose the right one for you. Just remember to *always* talk with your parents before you do *any* kind of investing with your money!

Savings Accounts

The most common way people invest is by putting money in a savings account at a bank.

RISK: None

MINIMUM $ NEEDED: $100 is often the minimum (however, banks may differ, so check with your own bank).

PLUS: Your money will grow automatically.

MINUS: The growth is very gradual.

How they work

You may think that when you put money in a bank, it just sits there. But a savings account is a risk-free way to make your money *grow*!

When you put your money in a bank (called *making a deposit*), the bank pays *you* for storing your money with them. The money the bank pays you is called *interest*. Banks need your money to give loans to other customers and to make their own investments. But all of that goes on behind the scenes, and any time you want to take your money out (called *withdrawing*, or *making a withdrawal*), it's guaranteed to be there. As long as your bank is FDIC-insured, your money is protected by the Federal Deposit Insurance Corporation. Ask your bank if it's covered by the FDIC, just to be safe!

Interest is often not a lot of money—but it adds up, because banks pay interest not only on the money you loan them, but on the *interest* you've earned. That's the beauty of it. If you invest, say, $100 in a bank that pays you 3% interest per year, you'll earn $3 at the end of the year. Next year, you'll earn 3% of $103 . . . and on and on and on. This is called *compound interest*. It's like getting free money without doing anything. Even if you never added more money to your original deposit, you'd continue to make money;

though of course, the more money you put into your account over time, the more interest you'd earn. To learn more about compound interest, try the compound interest calculator at EconEdLink (www.econedlink.org/lessons/em377).

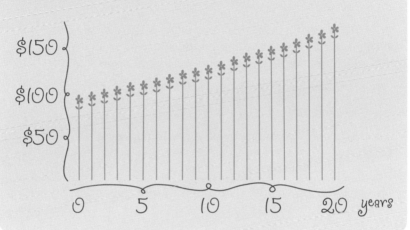

The Magic of Compound Interest

See how your money will grow over time with 3% compound interest.

$150

$100

$50

0   5   10   15   20 years

How to open a savings account

Most banks have special savings accounts for students to open jointly with a parent or guardian. Pick a time to go to the bank with a parent, and find out in advance what paperwork you may need to bring, like a birth certificate or Social Security card. When you're there, make sure the bank teller answers any questions you have, including:

- What is the minimum amount of money needed to open a savings account?

- Does the account always need to have at least a certain amount of money in it? What happens if you go below that minimum amount? Will there be any charges?

- What is the interest rate on the account?

- Are there any service fees?

- Are there any promotions or bonuses for opening an account now? (Sometimes banks offer free products or even money to new account holders.)

- Do you need a co-signer (like a parent or a guardian) for your account?

- Will you be given a "bank book" to track changes in your account? Can you check your account online?

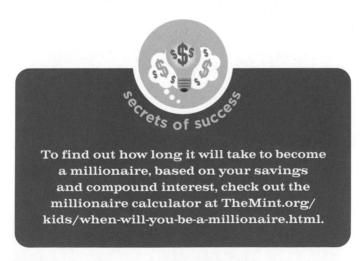

secrets of success

To find out how long it will take to become a millionaire, based on your savings and compound interest, check out the millionaire calculator at TheMint.org/kids/when-will-you-be-a-millionaire.html.

Other Savings Options at Banks

Some people invest in *online savings accounts* instead of, or in addition to, traditional savings accounts, because they often pay a higher interest rate.

With online savings accounts, you manage your account through the computer rather than going to an actual bank. Ask your bank if it offers online savings accounts. Also, talk to your parents about whether they'd be comfortable with your having one, or whether they'd prefer that you stick with a more traditional savings account.

Another option that's similar to a savings account is a certificate of deposit, or CD. CDs also often pay a higher interest rate; that's because CDs require you to leave your money with the bank for a set amount of time, ranging from a few months to several years, before you can withdraw your money and the interest it has earned.

secrets of success

You'll probably be given a receipt each time you make a deposit or withdraw money from your account. Keep your receipts together in a folder or shoebox and, in a small notebook or passbook (some banks supply these), keep track of your deposits and withdrawals. Or track them online.

Money's Many Forms

Other than saving accounts, three other banking terms you've probably heard about are *checks*, *ATM cards*, and *debit cards*. Here's the quick scoop on each.

CHECKS. A check is a paper certificate linked to someone's bank account (called a *checking account*). When you write a check for a certain amount of money, that money is automatically taken out of your checking account when the person who receives the check "cashes" it. You should *never* write a check for more money than you have in your checking account. If you do, the check will *bounce,* and you will be charged a fine by your bank. Checking accounts are most useful to people who have regular bills to pay, like rent or a telephone bill.

ATM CARDS. An ATM card is a plastic card linked directly to your savings and/or checking account. You can use it at an ATM (*automatic teller machine*) to take money from your account. Some ATM cards, are also *debit cards* (see below).

DEBIT CARDS. A debit card *looks* like a credit card, but it is connected directly to a checking account—and you can only use it to buy things up to the amount of money you have in your checking account. So if you have $100 in your checking account, you can use your debit card for up to $100; after that, your card will be declined at a store's cash register.

Savings Bonds

Another way to invest your money is by buying savings bonds.

RISK: Depends on the type of bond

MINIMUM $ NEEDED: $25 (for U.S. government bonds)

PLUS: Your money can grow more in the form of bonds than with savings accounts.

MINUS: You have to wait an extended amount of time before getting back your money plus its interest.

How they work

Buying a bond means giving money to a company or the government as a loan, for a set amount of time. When that time is over, you get your money back *plus* interest. Sometimes, bonds pay interest throughout the year, before their term is up. That money is called *dividends*. The date when you get your money and interest back is called the *maturity date*.

So, in money talk, a bond is an **investment** you make in a company or government organization. When the bond **matures**, you cash it in and get your original investment back plus **interest**. Some bonds pay interest throughout the year, instead of all at once—these payments are called **dividends**.

How much interest (or extra money) you get back varies by time and risk. The longer you agree to give your money to the company or government, the more they will pay you in interest. The riskier the bond, the higher the interest paid.

All bonds are given a "risk" grade, from A to C, where A is safe and C is risky. With risky bonds, there's no guarantee you'll ever get your original money back *or* make any interest. So why invest in risky bonds? Because when they *do* pay off, they pay a lot more money than safer bonds.

One type of very safe bond is a U.S. savings bond. When you loan money to the U.S. government through a bond, the government uses that money to pay its bills. To reward you, it *guarantees* to pay you back with interest. Depending on how long you agree to leave your money with them, your money can even double! The advantage bonds have is that you can buy them with as little as $25, and if you use the interest you make for your education, the government will reward you by not charging you any taxes on the interest. Bonds come in several dollar amounts, or *denominations,* like paper money does.

How to buy a savings bond

You can buy bonds at any age as long as you're a resident of the United States and have a Social Security number. You can buy basic U.S. bonds from your local bank or credit union. So once you get a parent's permission, call the bank where you or your family have a savings account, and tell them you'd like to buy a bond. Ask these questions:

- Do they have bonds?

- What is the minimum bond you can buy?

- What paperwork do you need to bring?

- When can you come in to buy one?

WHEN YOU ARRIVE AT THE BANK, ASK THESE QUESTIONS:

- How long will you have to wait to cash in your bond?

- Are there any penalties (fines) if you want to redeem your bond before it matures?

- How much interest will it earn over time?

When you leave, you'll be given a paper certificate. You'll need this certificate to cash in your bond later, so put it in a secure place, or ask a parent to hold it or keep it in a safe deposit box for you. When your bond matures, you can cash it in at most banks or credit unions. You can learn more about bonds using the resources listed on pages 94–95.

The Stock Market

A third way to invest your money is in the stock market.

RISK: High

MINIMUM $ NEEDED: Well, that depends on the stock, and whether you buy it through a stockbroker (a person trained and licensed to handle stock deals). Sometimes you have to pay a fee each time you invest money (in addition to the money you're investing). To help make sense of it all, read on to find out how you and your parent(s) can make the best investments for you!

PLUS: Investing wisely in the stock market can result in high rewards—and you have the potential to earn a lot of money on your investment.

MINUS: The stock market is risky—and you could lose a big portion of your investment.

How it works

When you look at the newspaper, you may not even look at the stock report section. And it's not hard to understand why: It can seem like a massive jumble of numbers and code words that have *nothing* to do with your life!

But to understand the stock market, it helps to think of it in terms of your own life. Imagine you want to start a company making hand-painted T-shirts, called Totally T-Shirt. To begin, you'd have to buy a bunch of plain T-shirts, fabric paint, and other supplies. These can get expensive, so you ask your parents for help. They give you money, and in return, you agree to give them some of the money you make when you sell the T-shirts. If your parents pay half of your expenses, you offer to give them half of the money you make (called your *profits*). If they pay one-fourth of your expenses, you give them one-fourth of your profits.

Your parents know there's no guarantee you'll sell any T-shirts at all. If you don't, they won't get any money back. But they believe in you, and they're willing to take the risk. They are your *investors,* because they are investing money in your business. They are giving you money in exchange for a *share* in your profits.

Now imagine that not just your parents, but *hundreds* of investors give money to your company in exchange for some of your profits. You sell them each a "share" of your business, like a piece of the pie. When you start your business, no one knows whether you're going to make money or not, so the risk is high and you have to sell the shares pretty cheaply. Let's say you start by charging them $1 per share.

The investors are hoping you'll be able to use their money to build up your business and make even more money. For example, you might use their money to buy an iron-on machine so you can make

T-shirts more quickly. The more money your business makes, the more money the investors get when you divide it up. The less money your business makes, the less they get. And if your business slows down or stops, they may make no money at all!

Think of the stock market as being made up of thousands of companies like Totally T-Shirt. Each one of these businesses wants investors to buy shares in their company, which are called *stock*.

A second important thing to understand is that the *value* of stock goes up or down depending on how well a company is doing. Let's say that Totally T-Shirt does well: One of your tees showed up on a popular website, and now everyone wants one. You're selling T-shirts faster than you can make them! As your business does better, more investors want to get involved. They all want a share and are willing to pay more to get one. Remember how you started by selling shares for $1 each? Now people will pay $100 for a share! The *value* of a share has gone way up.

So what does this mean for investors? How can you make money in the stock market? If you are an investor, you can make money (and lose money) simply by buying and selling your stocks. If you sell your stock as the value of a company goes *up,* you make money. If you sell your stock as the value of a company goes *down,* you might lose money. The more stock you own, the more you stand to make—or lose.

The investors (like your parents), who got in early on Totally T-Shirt and paid only $1 for a share, can now sell their share to someone else for $100 and make a $99 profit! Of course, it can also go the other way. Let's say your Uncle Charlie pays $100 for a share. But then you break your arm and can't make any more T-shirts. Your business stops doing well and no one wants to invest in it. The value of the shares plummets. The only buyer Uncle Charlie can find will pay a mere $10 for the share. So he's lost $90!

The actual stock market is more complicated than this example, but it follows the same general idea. So it's very important to remember that *you can lose money in the stock market—even all of it*. When you buy stock, the company doesn't guarantee you anything, and the government won't pay you back, either. (Plus, the government requires you to pay taxes on any money you make in the stock market.)

Anyone who invests in the stock market will want to read news about the company or companies they're investing in, and about current events and trends in general. Say you invest in a company that makes snow shovels. But then you hear a news report that there will be no snow all winter, which means no one will need shovels. You may want to sell your stock right away, before the value gets too low. Or if you own stock in a company that is doing really well, you may want to buy more shares of it *before* the stock price gets too high.

There are several stock markets—think of them as shopping malls, each with a different selection of stores. The biggest stock markets in the United States are the New York Stock Exchange (NYSE), the NASDAQ (an acronym that stands for National Association of Securities Dealers Automated Quotation system), and the American Stock Exchange (AMEX). You'll find all kinds of companies in these stock markets—from ones you know well, like Disney and Nike, to smaller companies, whose goods and services are less well-known.

secrets of success

One way to minimize risk when you invest is to not put all your money in one thing, but rather to spread it out over a mix of stocks and bonds. This is called *diversification*. Not every investment will do well at all times, so diversifying your money gives you a balance between investments that may be up or down. Some people choose to invest in *mutual funds*, which are a mix of stock and bonds.

Making Sense of Stock Listings

Whatever company you buy stock in, you can track how much your stock is worth online (at various sites) or in the newspaper. Stock listings look a little different from one website or newspaper to the next, but generally look something like this make-believe example for Totally T-Shirt. Wherever you decide to track stock listings, there should be a key to explain the symbols and numbers.

STOCK	OPEN	HIGH	LOW	52 WK-RANGE
TTS	$94.50	$95	$94.25	$70 – $100

STOCK The symbol for the company.

OPEN The price the stock opened at in the morning.

HIGH The highest price of the day.

LOW The lowest price of the day.

52 WK-RANGE The range of prices of the stock over the last year.

How to buy stocks

Here are two ways to get your feet wet in the stock market.

1. Try (risk-free!) "mock" investing. Many schools around the country participate in mock stock markets, also known as *stock market simulations*. Students are given fake money to "invest" in the stock market to track over a set amount of time. This way, they can learn how current events and trends affect the decisions they make about investing.

To get your school involved, go to your math or social studies teacher or guidance counselor and suggest the idea. Tell him or her that you think a stock market lesson would be a fun, hands-on way to learn about economics and current events. Then, have him or her check out The Stock Market Game (stockmarketgame.org) for information about setting one up.

Even if your school doesn't participate, there are other stock market simulations you can take part in on your own. Some of them even award scholarships to the students who win! Talk to your guidance counselor or a parent to find the right one for you.

2. Try *real* investing *with a parent*. You have to be at least 18 to buy stock on your own, but a parent or guardian can set up a stock account *for* you, with the adult acting as a "custodian." This means that your parents are the actual behind-the-scenes owners of the stock—they can choose to sell it at any time.

Before you ask your parents to buy stock in your name, it's a good idea to track the progress of the stocks you think you'd like to buy. You can choose from thousands of stocks from both big and small companies.

News about new companies, changes at old companies, and new product developments should all weigh in when you choose your stocks. Make a list of the companies you are interested in, and then visit each company's media page for press releases announcing new products and activities. Be sure to keep an eye out for articles and updates on the companies you have selected.

After a few months of tracking your stocks, you and your parent can buy the stocks you want by contacting a stockbroker or a trusted online broker.

A FINAL NOTE

When you invest your money, you can make it grow more than it would if it just sat in your piggy bank. But investing can be risky—and the only way to find out whether it's safer to keep your money in your ol' piggy or to start investing is to talk with a parent and do some research together. Or you can get the help of a financial expert.

Learning about investing—and figuring out the right kind of investments for *you*—can change your life, and your future, forever.

hey, big

spender!

Sure, saving and investing pay off. But it's not bad to *spend* some of your money, too. Shopping is *fun*, and a little "retail pick-me-up" can totally make your day.

The trick to becoming a smart spender isn't to worry about every penny you spend—it's figuring out how to make your money go as *far* as possible, and what's *really* worth spending money on in the first place! That way, you can still have fun shopping without blowing your bigger-picture money plans. This chapter will help you figure out what kind of spender you are, where all your money is going, and how you can start getting more for your money.

What Kind of Spender Are You?

START HERE

What do you do with your birthday money?

SPEND IT!

SAVE HALF, AND SPEND HALF.

SAVE IT!

For friends birthdays, you:

You know how much money is in your wallet:

MAKE THEM SOMETHING

APPROXIMATELY

BUY THEM SOMETHING

You shop:

DOWN TO THE LAST CENT

EVERY DAY

AS LITTLE AS POSSIBLE

When you want something, you:

A FEW TIMES A MONTH

You buy new clothes when:

BUY IT

RESEARCH YOUR OPTIONS

YOU WANT THEM

YOU NEED THEM

PAMPERED POOCH You've got an eye for style and you love to indulge. But remember: Although treating yourself can be fun, there are other (free!) ways to have a good time. And if you save your money now, you'll have more of it later, for more important things.

BALANCED BEE You think before reaching for your wallet, but you're not afraid to spend, either. Since you already have your spending in check, you're ready to start working with a parent to become an active investor, using the tips in the previous chapter.

FRUGAL FROGGY It's important not to spend your money as soon as you get it. But remember that it's not bad to spend *some* of your money, too. And the best way to become comfortable spending is to come up with, and stick to, a simple plan. Check out page 34, and soon you'll be on your way to saving *and* spending on your own terms.

Where Does Your Money Go?

Does this sound familiar? You start a typical week with, say, $20 in your wallet and, by Wednesday, realize it's practically gone—*without* anything major to show for it.

It just seems to *happen* that you spend a dollar here (on gum), $5 there (on a magazine)—and before you know it, you've spent so much that you can't afford the things you really want (clothes! music! DVDs!) by the time the weekend comes around.

To make your money go farther, you have to first figure out where it's going. Copy the chart on the next page into your notebook or onto a sheet of paper (copy it seven times, once for each day in the week). Then, for one week, use it to keep track of *everything* you buy each day. Be honest! Record each purchase right after you buy it—don't wait until the end of the day or you might forget something. Say whether it was something you *needed* or just wanted, whether it was a "little," "middle," or "big" purchase (relative to *your* spending budget), and how much it cost. In addition to making a list of your purchases, it's also a good idea to keep receipts (they'll help you keep track of your spending, and you'll probably need a receipt if you want to return or exchange anything).

Day of the Week:

ITEM	NEED, OR WANT?	LITTLE, MIDDLE, BIG?	COST
1.			
2.			
3.			
4.			
5.			
6.			
7.			
8.			
9.			
10.			

After the seventh day, add it all up. Then answer the following:

- How much did you spend this week?

- Were most of your purchases needs, or wants? (Think about it . . . did you really need them?) Did you notice any patterns to how you spend your money (i.e., where and when you tend to spend your money)?

- Could you have gone without buying some of the items on your list without your life changing dramatically?

- Could you cut back on at least half of your wants, or one-quarter of them?

The point isn't to make you feel bad every time you spend money. It's just to show you that if you're more *aware* of your spending habits, you'll see how changing just a few of them could lead to big changes in your wallet!

It's the Little Things

Look back at the things on your list you marked as "little." These are the things you probably don't think twice about—the bottled water, the magazines, the movie popcorn.

Some of these might brighten your day and bring you momentary happiness—and that's important! But little things *can* add up and keep you from getting other things you *really* want. So here are some tips to keep the little things . . . little!

BANISH BOREDOM. Waiting on line at a store can be boring, and you might find yourself reaching for magazines or candy you hadn't planned on buying. Instead, keep yourself occupied by listening to your mp3 player or try just looking at your favorite magazine while in line and then put it back on the rack.

GO GENERIC. Always consider cheaper alternatives to brand names.

GIVE YOURSELF A DAILY "LITTLE THINGS" BUDGET. Tell yourself that you won't spend more than, say, $3 a day on unplanned purchases like snacks or gum or soda.

SAVE YOUR CHANGE. See what happens when you don't use your change. Only use *bills* to buy little things, then put aside any change you get for your savings. You'll be surprised by how it adds up!

GO ONE DAY WITHOUT SPENDING ANY MONEY. Then, see how you feel. Did you really miss buying anything in particular? That is probably a clue about what's most important to you. Keep that in mind when you start spending again.

The Middle Riddle

Look again at your list—what did you mark as the "middle" stuff? Clothing, accessories, gadgets, and going out probably fall into this category for you.

This can be the trickiest category, because the costs are high enough to affect your budget, but low enough to seem harmless at that critical moment. You're probably faced with tons of "middle-cost" options all the time, trying to keep up with trends—or your friends.

The best way to decide whether to buy something like this is to do a quick "cost-benefit analysis" in your head. That may sound overly technical and dorky, but all it means is that you ask yourself whether the happiness you'd get from spending your money *now* is more important than having that money *later*. In other words, each time you find yourself reaching for your wallet to pay for a new sweater or pair of earrings, *stop,* and ask yourself these questions:

1. Do I need this, or do I want this?

2. Do I want this because of what other people will think of it—or because of what *I* think of it?

3. Will I still want this a week from now? A month from now? A year from now?

4. Do I have enough money in my budget for this? If not, could I share with or borrow this from a friend or sibling instead of buying it?

5. Is there a store that charges less for the same thing, or an upcoming sale or coupon I could wait for?

6. What other things *can't* I buy if I buy this? Is this worth giving up those things?

If you ask yourself all those questions and still come to *yes,* then it's a smart purchase.

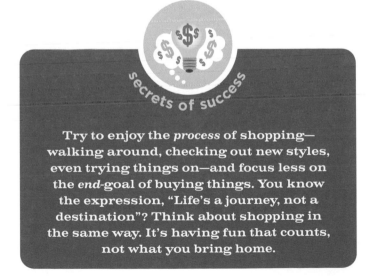

secrets of success

Try to enjoy the *process* of shopping—walking around, checking out new styles, even trying things on—and focus less on the *end*-goal of buying things. You know the expression, "Life's a journey, not a destination"? Think about shopping in the same way. It's having fun that counts, not what you bring home.

Beating the Urge to Splurge

There's a reason shopping is called "retail therapy"—sometimes spending money can give you a quick pick-me-up.

But indulgent spending can be a waste of money that later you'll wish you had. So when a spending pang hits, try one of these "therapeutic" alternatives.

HOLD A CLOTHING SWAP. Everyone gets tired of their clothes. But instead of running out to buy *new* clothes, invite your friends over and ask everyone to bring clothes they're willing to trade. Put the clothes in a pile and have everyone choose a number from a hat. The person with the lowest number picks what they want first. The next lowest number goes after her. Continue until everyone's had a chance to swap something.

VOLUNTEER. Working to help other people can make you feel good about yourself in a way that money can't. Consider volunteering at a charity or organization that does work you value.

EXERCISE, SING, DANCE. Remind yourself of all of the things you love to do that don't cost a dime!

SEE THE WORLD. Or at least see how far your money would take you in different parts of the world. Go to Exchange-Rates.org to see how far a dollar would get you in cities ranging from Zurich to Hong Kong!

HIT THE BOOKS. With so many great bookstores around these days, it's easy to forget how much fun the ol' library can be. Libraries don't just have dusty reference books—they have magazines, CDs, and DVDs you can borrow for free!

The Big Time

Things like cars, sweet sixteen parties, computers, and college are major expenses that should be considered very, very carefully. Here are some ways to ensure you make the best choices.

DO YOUR RESEARCH. The library and the Internet—and your local librarians—are great resources for *anything* you may be researching.

TALK TO OTHERS WHO'VE MADE THE SAME CHOICES. Before you spend your hard-earned money, talk to people who've been through this decision to find out how they feel about the choices they made. Did that car work out well? Do they like the college they chose? How does their computer work? Friends and family are likely to be more honest than salespeople, after all!

COMPARISON SHOP. Always look around to make sure you're getting the best deal for your money.

A FINAL NOTE

Spending your money wisely—only splurging on things you *really* want—will make the stuff you buy that much more special and will keep you in control of your finances.

When you start spending money that you earned, and not money from your parents, you'll want to make sure that your money goes as far as it possibly can!

taking

CREDIT CARD

123 456 7890 123

charge

When you were younger, you may have seen adults using credit cards and thought to yourself: *"Wow—you can use a little piece of plastic instead of money to buy whatever you want?!"*

Maybe you even played "store," and you and your friends pretended to buy things using fake credit cards. But as you probably know by now, paying for stuff on a credit card doesn't mean it's free, it just means that you have to pay for it *later.* The reality is that credit cards are useful—and can be powerful—but they're not magic.

When you learn how they really work and how to use them wisely, credit cards *can* become an important part of your financial toolbox. But credit cards also come with big risks, and it's important to learn the good stuff *and* the dangerous stuff about them. That way, your credit cards won't take control of you, and any time you say "Charge it!" *you'll* be the one in charge.

The Power of Plastic

So what *is* credit, anyway?

Think of it as a temporary loan—a credit card company (like Visa or MasterCard, or American Express) covers the cost of your purchases, with the expectation that you'll pay them back. (When you're under 18, the only way you can use a credit card is if a parent gets you one with both of your names on it.)

So one good thing about a credit card is that it can be more convenient to carry one around than to keep wads of cash in your wallet. And if you're in another country, it's often less of a hassle to have a credit card than to have to trade in your U.S. dollars for the local money (or *currency*). Credit cards can also be useful in case of emergencies, if you need more money than you have on you (and no, shopping doesn't count as an emergency!).

It can also be *safer* to use a credit card than cash: Any time you buy something with a credit card, your credit card keeps a computerized record of your purchase. This record can be used to prove how much you paid for something, and you can always call your credit card company if you think a store accidentally (or intentionally!) charged you too much for something when you weren't paying attention. If you buy something that is defective, credit card companies will stand behind you, and the charge can be erased from your account. Plus, if you ever lose your credit card, you can call the credit card company and tell them to cancel your account to make sure no one else finds it and uses it. If someone else does charge something to your account, you won't have to pay for it, as long as you tell the company what is happening. In these ways, having a credit card is like having a financial support system to back you up. You can't say the same for cash: Once cash is out of your hands, there's no way to prove how much you had. And if your cash gets stolen or lost, there's no one you can call—you're simply, and unfortunately, out of luck.

Another good thing about credit cards is that they prepare you for your future. See, the minute you have your *own* credit card (and not one that's tied to your parents), something called a *credit report* will be started for you. It's like a report card of how well you manage your money: If you always pay your credit card bill on time, you'll have a good grade. If you always pay it late (more on that later!), you'll have a bad grade. Your credit grade is a public report, and it will later be used by banks, car companies, and real estate agents to decide whether they will let you buy things like homes and cars. This may seem like a *long* way off—but your credit report starts as *soon* as you have your own credit card, and it's not something you can hide. It's important to have a credit report so that you have a public record of being financially responsible (if you don't have *any* credit report, it could be harder for you to make big purchases later on down the road). So it's *really* important for you to be smart about using your credit card. It can be a huge asset later in life, or it can come back to haunt you: *You* have the power to control what your credit report says about you!

Another kind of plastic

A **PREPAID DEBIT** or **CHECK CARD** is different from a credit card, even though it may be issued by a credit card company like Visa or American Express. It's actually more like a gift certificate that's sponsored by a credit card company and that you can use anywhere. If you receive one as a gift, remember that it represents the amount of money listed on it—keep it in a safe place, and spend it wisely.

The Danger Zone

It's important to have a good credit report, but it's not always easy. To understand why, it helps to make sense of how credit card companies make their money.

After all, you've probably been wondering: *What's in it for the credit card companies—and why would they just offer to loan people money?*

Well, it works like this: Credit cards come with a limit on how much you can spend (called a *credit limit,* or *credit line*)—but that amount is *not* tied to how much money you actually have. That's where credit cards can become dangerous—and where credit card companies make their money. If you sign up for a credit card that will let you spend up to $2,000, and you go out and buy $2,000 worth of stuff but you don't actually *have* $2,000, you won't be able to pay back the credit card company on time. That's where the trouble starts.

Remember when you learned about earning interest—when a bank pays you for loaning them money? Well, with credit cards, it works the *other* way: you are taking out a loan from a credit card company, and if you can't pay it back immediately, you'll have to pay the credit card company interest (in *addition* to the money you spent on your purchases).

Each month, you'll receive a bill from the credit card company, listing the things you bought and the amount you owe. If you can pay the entire amount by the payment deadline, you're in the clear. But if you can't pay the entire amount, the credit card company will charge you interest. The more money you owe, the more they'll charge. This means you could end up paying more for the stuff you bought than it cost in the first place! And even if you stop using your credit card altogether for a little while, the interest charges will keep getting higher and higher (*compounding*). Even worse, there's also a penalty fee for being late on your payment, even by a day. And *that's* how credit card companies make money: They know that people will buy more than they can afford, and that they won't be able to pay their entire bill. Americans owe billions of dollars to credit card companies! Owing money means having debt or being in debt. It becomes a vicious cycle, and the only way to avoid it is to make sure it doesn't start in the first place. So always remember: Credit card charges represent real money—and you should never buy something on your credit card that you know you can't afford with cash.

family affair

Ask a parent to show you one of their credit card statements and to explain the different parts of it to you.

Taking control

Credit cards aren't the problem—it's how people often *use* them (or abuse them) and rack up debt that leads to the drama!

Imagine you didn't turn in your homework one day at school. But instead of just being reprimanded by your teacher, she decides to follow you around school, call you at home, send letters to your house, e-mail you, tell the principal, your parents, and everyone at school, so that pretty soon you start to feel like you just can't escape. Well, that's how it can feel when debt starts piling up—it can haunt you.

So here's how you can avoid credit card catastrophes:

WATCH YOUR SPENDING. Never charge more on your credit card than you actually have set aside in your budget for spending. A lot of people see credit cards as a way to buy nice things now that they don't have the money to pay for in their bank account. But that's how the trouble starts! So look at your bank account, and talk to your parents about *exactly* how much you can spend using your credit card.

PAY YOUR BILL ON TIME. You will be charged a fine each time your bill is late, and your lateness will also be noted on your credit report.

PAY THE COMPLETE AMOUNT OF YOUR BILL. Credit card bills are confusing. They tell you that you can pay a *minimum amount*. What they *don't* tell you is that if you pay less than the full amount, you'll be charged interest. While you must pay the minimum amount to continue to have a good credit rating, it's best if you can pay off the entire bill and avoid spending your money on interest.

NEVER GIVE YOUR CREDIT CARD NUMBER OUT TO ANYONE.
Ever. Now that people can buy things on the Internet or over the phone using just a credit card, you'll want to make sure no one but you and your parents know your credit card number. Never give it out over the phone, and don't buy anything online without *first* asking your parents' permission.

CHOOSE CASH. See how long you can go without using your credit card, and use only cash to buy things. When you rely on cash, you simply can't spend more money than you have!

DON'T HAVE MORE THAN ONE CREDIT CARD. Credit card companies are constantly trying to tempt students into signing up for cards by offering free bonuses like T-shirts. But if you're going to have a credit card, have just one for now—it'll be challenging enough to manage that without worrying about juggling *more* than one.

KNOW THE LINGO. Credit card applications and bills can be full of confusing terms. The Federal Trade Commission (FTC) has a website that explains them (www.ftc.gov/bcp/conline/pubs/credit/choose.shtm). You may want to ask your parents to go over the site with you.

And remember: Most major stores and restaurants and companies will accept credit cards, but some places don't. Find out before you go to buy something whether they'll accept credit cards.

A FINAL NOTE

Credit cards may seem like fun and games, but they're a huge responsibility with long-term consequences.

If you have a credit card now or are getting one in the future, learn *everything* you can about your particular card—and use it *wisely!*

mishaps

Everyone's been in a sticky money situation at *some* point.

Perhaps you loaned money to a friend and didn't get it back, or someone at school asked you how much money your parents make, or you have no idea how much to tip your waitress—the list goes on and on. Luckily, this chapter will show you how to get through those awkward moments without costing you a dime, or your friendships.

scenario: You just had a meal or got your hair cut, and you're not sure how much to tip the server or stylist.

solution: It's normal to tip 15% of your bill, but great service usually deserves a 20% tip. To figure out how much 20% is, move the decimal point of your bill to the left once. Then, double the number. So if your bill before tax is $40.00, move the decimal over once to get $4.00, then double it to get $8.00.

scenario: You and your friends go out to eat, and you order way less than everyone else. So when the bill comes, you don't want to be expected to split it evenly.

solution: The next time you go out to eat, ask the waitress for a separate check when she takes your order. If your friends give you weird looks, say, "I only have a certain amount of money on me, and I want to make sure I don't overspend." If your friends see that your intentions are good and you're actually trying to avoid drama later, they should appreciate your effort and not make a big deal.

scenario: Someone asks how much you paid for something—and you feel awkward telling them.

solution: Say, "Aw, it makes me feel so weird to talk about stuff like that—I'd rather not."

scenario: You get teased at school for wearing or using a generic version of a brand-name item, like sneakers or food.

solution: Teasing can be hurtful, and you should always talk to a guidance counselor or parent if someone is emotionally, verbally, or physically abusing you. As hard as it may be, the quickest way to get people to stop teasing you is to not give them any kind of reaction or sign that they're affecting you. It takes strength and courage to ignore bullies, and it will be hard—especially if, deep down, you would like to have brand-name styles. But know this: While brand-name luxuries can make you feel good for a fleeting moment, you don't *need* them. If you want to make your clothes more unique and exciting, turn them into one-of-a-kind, do-it-yourself projects using paint, beads, and fabric or by cutting and sewing them to fit you just right! Your library will have books on craft projects, and you can always turn to fashion magazines for inspiration.

scenario: You loaned money to a friend, and she hasn't paid you back.

solution: You don't want to create tension between you and your friend or make her feel uncomfortable, but you deserve to get paid back. The next time you see her, bring up the money she owes you by telling her why you need it back. For example, say, "Hey, I owe my sister for a gift she got our mom—can you please pay me back so I can give her the money?" Or simply say, "I know talking about money is weird, and I don't mean to make you feel uncomfortable, but I need the money I loaned you back."

In the future, avoid lending anyone money. Often, it leads to nothing but drama! And if you are going to lend money to a friend, make sure you talk about (and agree on) when you'll be repaid *beforehand.*

scenario: You want to attend a school-related event like a dance or school trip, but you don't have enough money.

solution: Ask your guidance counselor if your school has any programs to help you attend school events. For dances, consider buying a vintage dress from a secondhand store and adding favorite accessories to give it a personal spin. Also, check out www.mypromdress.org for new or gently-worn prom dresses for only $5. Your guidance counselor might also be able to help you find a short-term job that will let you earn enough money to cover the cost of the trip or dress.

scenario: Someone says something judgmental or obnoxious about an expensive item you or your family own—and you feel self-conscious about it.

solution: It can be hard for people to sympathize with families who seem to have a lot of money. What they don't understand is that having money can come with the same amount of problems and awkwardness as *not* having money! If someone makes a rude, nosy, or judgmental comment about your family's money, try to ignore them or change the subject. If it's someone you're close to, tell them it makes you uncomfortable to be judged for something you have no control over. No one chooses what kind of family they're born into, after all.

secrets of success

There are tons of online scams out there. To avoid them, never reply to an e-mail from a stranger, and don't give out your e-mail address, phone number, or credit card number to anyone online, *ever*.

A FINAL NOTE

Money drama can be stressful and even downright depressing!

Face money problems as soon as they crop up instead of letting them drag on. This will help you to feel in control, and you will learn valuable lessons for the future.

the final exam

Now that you know the tricks for making, saving, investing, and spending your money, it's time to take charge of your own financial plan!

So take your magic wand (okay, your pen) and get started with this worksheet. Copy this page twelve times so that you have one sheet for each month of the year. The first day of every month, fill out the squares with your money plan for that month, and then do your best to *stick to it!*

Month _____

Expected Income $ _____
(from allowance, working, gifts, and other stuff)

Spending

This month, I'll keep
$ _____
for spending money.

Here is one spending habit
I will change this month:

_____
_____
_____
_____
_____

Saving (Short-term)

This month, I'll put
$ _____
in a savings or other type of
interest-bearing account toward
my #1 savings goal.

My current savings goal is:
$ _____
Total amount I need to save:
$ _____
How much I've already
saved $ _____
How much more I need to
save $ _____

Saving (Long-term)

This month, I'll ask my
parents to help me invest:
$ _____

I want to invest the money
in the following places:

Savings bonds: $ _____

Stock market: $ _____

Other: $ _____

_____
_____

Charity

This month, I'll put aside
$ _____
to give to charity.

The top three charities I want to
learn more about are:

_____
_____
_____
_____
_____

DONATIONS
City Food Bank

extra credit!

Learning about money isn't always a hoot, but the more fun you have with it, the more inspired you'll be to think about it! So now it's time to kick back and relax.

Q&A

Sometimes, the best way to learn about money is right in front of you. Take time to "interview" your friends and family about their money habits. Don't pry into private matters like how much money they make, but do ask them what their first job was, what their favorite job was, what their savings tips are, and what they splurge on. Ask for their best piece of money advice. Then write it all down here or on another piece of paper. You'll get a whole new set of tips and tricks, as well as learning some new things about your friends and family!

_____

_____

_____

_____

_____

_____

_____

_____

_____

WORD SEARCH

Can you find all the money words in this puzzle? Look up, down, across, diagonally—and backwards!

ALLOWANCE, BOND, CHECKS, CREDIT CARD, INTEREST, JOB INTERVIEW, MONEY, RÉSUMÉ, SAVING, SCHOLARSHIP, STOCK, TAXES

```
O N S H I P A X X A L N N I S
B A I R L E C N A W O L L A K
R R W E I V R E T N I B O J L
C A A S V D R S O J M P J A S
L O L E E O N S C T A B A H
I O L R U J E O K J K A J L P
V T S E X A T X B E M C T L B
I S T N T S E R E T N I E W O
E L R I Y R Y E N O M X X H N
E L E B R R S S A V I N G P C
W A E J E E U U L Y E E N M K
M O T I N T M M L E X A A C O
D R A C T I D E R C S J O B C
B O E N A A W O L M E T P M S
P I H S R A L O H C S L X X T
```

(answers on page 93)

Time Capsule

Time plays a major role when it comes to money. Over time, your savings will grow, you'll make more and more interest, you'll learn how to manage your money better, and you'll figure out your priorities. That's why it will be fascinating ten years from now to see how far you've come! To give yourself some perspective (and some laughs) in ten years, make a money time capsule.

1. Find an old shoebox.

2. Put a copy of your current money plan from page 89 and a copy of your Wish List from page 41 inside. Also write a list of your money-related goals—what job do you hope you will have in ten years? How much money do you hope to be making in ten years? What is the one thing you love splurging on these days? Then, jot down a list of how much it costs to buy the things you use on a regular basis: How much does a movie cost? Jeans? Shoes? A slice of pizza? Toilet paper? Notebooks? It will be fun to see how much—or how little—prices change over ten years.

3. Seal the box with heavy-duty tape and write "Private!" on it.

4. Ask a parent to hold onto it for ten years or to give it to you when you graduate from college. Or tuck it away in the bottom of your closet, where you'll forget about it for the next decade!

```
O N S H I P A X X A L N N I S
B A I R L E C N A W O L L A K
R R W E I V R E T N I B O J L
C A A S V D R S O J M P J A S
L O L E E O N S C S T A B A H
I O L R U J E O K J K A J L P
V T S E X A T X B E M C T L B
I S T N T S E R E T N I E W O
E L R I Y R Y E N O M X X H N
E L E B R R S S A V I N G P C
W A E J E E U U L Y E E N M K
M O T I N T M M L E X A A C O
D R A C T I D E R C S J O B C
B O E N A A W O L M E T P M S
P I H S R A L O H C S L X X T
```

additional resources: the 411

There are *tons* of amazing money-related websites out there. Here are some of the most useful government and nonprofit sites—many of which were used during the research of this book.

BUREAU OF THE PUBLIC DEBT
For info on savings bonds
www.publicdebt.treas.gov/sav/sbkglosa.htm

CHOOSE TO SAVE
For general information on money and saving
www.choosetosave.org

FEDERAL RESERVE
For general info on money
www.federalreserve.gov/kids

FEDERAL TRADE COMMISSION
For info on credit cards
www.ftc.gov

GIRL SCOUTS MONEY$MARTS
For general money info
www.girlscouts.org/moneysmarts

GIRLSHEALTH.GOV
For info on planning for the future
Girlshealth.gov

HIGH SCHOOL FINANCIAL PLANNING PROGRAM FROM THE NATIONAL ENDOWMENT FOR FINANCIAL EDUCATION
For general money info
www.nefe.org

INTERNAL REVENUE SERVICE
For info on taxes
www.irs.gov